SCHOLASTIC'S
A+ JUNIOR GUIDE
TO TAKING TESTS

**Other A+ Junior Guides for You
by Louise Colligan**

Scholastic's A+ Junior Guide to Good Writing
Scholastic's A+ Junior Guide to Studying
Scholastic's A+ Junior Guide to Book Reports
Scholastic's A+ Junior Guide to Giving a Speech

SCHOLASTIC'S A+ JUNIOR GUIDE TO TAKING TESTS

LOUISE COLLIGAN

SCHOLASTIC INC.
New York Toronto London Auckland Sydney

ISBN 0-590-43148-X

12 11 10 9 8 7 6 5 4   1 2 3 4 5/9

Printed in the U.S.A.   40

First Scholastic printing, September 1990

TABLE OF CONTENTS

1
Step by Step to Super Tests

Pencil chewing. Nail biting. Uncontrollable butterflies. Are these some of the symptoms you get when your teacher announces a test? If you're like most students, you probably dread test days, as well as the days right before them when you'd rather do *anything* — even clean your room — than study!

Now that you're in the middle grades, you've probably noticed that hardly a week goes by without some kind of test. And they're not just the simple spelling and math quizzes you took in the lower grades. From now on, you'll probably face all kinds of tests — everything from multiple-choice tests to those with questions you have to answer in several paragraphs.

That's the bad news. The good news is you're probably so new at taking tests that you don't have too many bad habits yet. The middle-grade years are the perfect time to learn some simple skills to help you become a super test taker now and in the grades ahead.

The other good news is that successful test takers don't necessarily know the most, but they do know how to *make the most* of what they know. This means you don't have to memorize your whole math book or know every history date. To be a good test taker, you don't have to be super smart; you just have to *work* smart.

When it comes to tests, the surest way to avoid panic, cramming, and heart pounding is to follow the old scout's motto: BE PREPARED. Now you probably knew this before you even opened this book. But if you're like a lot of students, *preparing* often means worrying, losing sleep, stuffing your brain with facts, and forgetting about having a normal life until the big test is over.

This book will show you that getting yourself test-ready is a lot easier than that. Test taking is like any skill; there are a lot of small, steady, and painless steps you can take way ahead of the big event that will boost your chances of success. And many of these steps don't even involve studying!

After you read this book, keep it handy. At test time, use the Table of Contents and the Index to locate just the sections you need for the particular kind of test you're scheduled to take.

Working Smart Every Day

Before you learn about specific test skills, let's review a few simple things you can do to keep yourself test-ready all year long.

• *Keep a notebook for each of your subjects.* Usually teachers want you to have a three-ring binder with subject dividers. This is the best place to store your notes, homework, and class handout sheets.

• *Be equipped.* Keep track of upcoming tests on a calendar at home or one you carry right inside your binder. Stock a couple of extra pens, pencils, and some paper in your binder or in your locker or cubby so that you're always ready for class. Here are a few other supplies that will come in handy at test time: a highlighter for marking important parts of your notes, clips or those little yellow stick-on notes for locating textbook information quickly, a tape recorder and a blank tape to help you memorize facts.

• *Take notes when your teacher tells you to.* Luckily in the middle grades teachers do a lot of notetaking for you, either on the board or in class handouts. If something is written on the board, it's important, so copy it down. If you get a handout sheet, put it into the right section of your notebook.

• *Date your notes.* This way you won't wind up studying your rock and mineral notes from the week before when you're supposed to be reviewing this week's material on electricity.

• *Catch up right away.* Don't wait until a test is announced to make up missing work. If you're absent or late, see your teacher immediately to get missing notes and homework, or call a classmate to see what you missed. Arrange a time to make up tests you skipped. If you fall behind in your reading, catch up the very next weekend when your work load is probably light.

• *Save all your old tests.* Even if you think they belong at the bottom of your locker or in a wastebasket, old tests tell you a lot about yourself and the kinds of mistakes you tend to make. Maybe you know the information but keep misunderstanding the directions. This means you don't have to study harder — you just have to read directions more carefully. Maybe you work too fast or too slowly and should plan your test time more carefully.

Old tests will also help you see your teacher's testing style. Maybe he or she favors essay tests over multiple choice, which may mean you have to study differently. Maybe your teacher wants more of your *opinions* in essay answers and not just a rerun of facts from the book. Having your old tests in front of you is like getting a preview of an upcoming test. Keep these tests on hand all year long.

These few good habits will not only help at test time, they will help you become a more active, involved student every day.

Working Smart at Test Time

Day-by-day attention to notetaking, homework, and reading is the best study plan you can have for any test. If your work is up-to-date, you've already done most of the preparation you need before a test. Here are some other steps you can take in order to do the best possible job on your next big exam.

In-Class Countdown

1. *Write down the test date in your assignment book.* Mark the test date in big colored letters so you can't miss it. In the spaces before the test date, write down "Study for test" so that you remember to work a little bit each day.

2. *Write down what the test is going to cover.* Find out from your teacher the material the test will cover — a whole history unit or just one chapter? Fractions or decimals or both? See if you can find out from your teacher just what sort of test will be given. In Chapter 3, you will learn about all kinds of tests, from fill-in to essay tests. There are specific ways to prepare for each type.

3. *Listen for hints about the test.* In the days before a big test, most teachers review the material that the test will cover. This is the time to take good notes and underline or highlight whatever your teacher keeps repeating.

4. *See your teacher about anything you don't understand.* Sometimes it's hard for students who need help to ask for it. If you are not comfortable about asking questions in front of the whole class, see if you can catch your teacher at another time to answer any questions you have about the upcoming test or about material you don't understand. Maybe one more explanation of that science step or that word problem is all you need to remember it for good. When your teacher corrects your test later on, he or she is likely to remember and appreciate that you came for help on your own.

At-Home Countdown

1. *Copy your test date on a calendar.* Test reminders should go right up there with birthday parties, soccer practice, and doctors' appointments.

2. *Plan a study schedule.* No matter how many weeks you have to study for a test, break the job into small steps you can do a little at a time. Short study spurts help you remember material a lot more than squeezing all the work into one or two nights. You will find a week-long Study Planner on pages 82–83 of this book. See if you can get someone to

make you extra copies to fill out for any big tests you have. Here is how to plan for a big test a week away:

7–6 DAYS AHEAD:

• Catch up on any reading you haven't done.

• Borrow notes for any days you were out of school.

• Gather together all your old homework and old tests in one place and look them over.

5–4 DAYS AHEAD:

• Read over all your class notes and the teacher's handout sheets at least twice. Underline or highlight what looks important.

• Read the Table of Contents, the boldface headings, and chapter-end questions in your textbook.

3 DAYS AHEAD:

• Make up study tools like those shown in Chapter 2. These can include flash cards, question lists, outlines, summaries, and study tapes. To make up any study tool, go through your notes and textbook material and find ideas and facts you think the teacher might ask about. To make the job easy, just use single words or short phrases to sum up information.

2 DAYS AHEAD:

• Memorize the information in your study tools. You will learn the best ways to memorize on page 79.

1 DAY BEFORE THE TEST:

• Practice what you memorized. Spend extra time on items you still have problems with.

• Reread highlighted or underlined parts of your notes, textbook headings, and any material you clipped or noted with slips of paper.

• Pretest yourself. Ask yourself all the questions listed in your textbook and the questions you created in your study tools. Answer them in your head, out loud, or have someone quiz you.

• Line up whatever materials you need for the test. Double check that you have sharpened pencils with good erasers, working pens, scrap paper, and any books your teacher said to bring in.

• Get a good night's sleep. The great thing about working steadily all year long and studying for tests a little at a time is that you can relax and go to bed at your regular time. Rested and relaxed students make good test takers.

Test Day Countdown

1. *Eat a good breakfast.* This will give you plenty of energy for the test.

2. *Review your study tools.* You can skip this step if it makes you too nervous. Since you've done a lot of work already, there's no need to stuff yourself with last-minute information and get yourself nervous or tense. If you feel that happening, put all your materials away and forget about doing any

8

more work. What you've learned all along is going to help you a lot more than any last-minute cramming.

3. *Get to class a little early so you're not rushed.* Take a few deep breaths and let them out slowly as you wait for the teacher to hand out the test. If you feel jittery, tighten your toes or fingers and relax them very slowly. Picture a peaceful scene in your mind — water flowing slowly downstream, a warm breeze touching your face, golden sunlight spreading over you.

4. *Listen carefully to your teacher.* Find out how much time you have for the test and the value of the questions. Know *exactly* what you're supposed to do. Does the teacher want you to print or use script? Should you use a pen or a pencil? Can you use scrap paper? Ask your teacher to repeat any directions you may not be sure about.

5. *Read the directions twice.* Star or underline important parts of the directions, especially information about the time and value of the questions.

6. *Schedule your time.* If your teacher said the test will last a half hour and you have twenty questions each worth the same amount, give yourself a minute or so to answer each question. Then use the remaining ten minutes to review your answers or go back to any questions you may have skipped. Plan more time for more valuable sections of the test.

7. *Skim the whole test to get a sense of it.*

8. *Work on the easiest, most valuable questions first.* This will give you quick points and build up your self-confidence for the harder questions later on. Put a dot or a question mark in the margin for any questions you skip so that you will know where to return when you complete the easier questions. *Keep moving.* The idea is to gain points for what you do know.

9. *Guess answers.* Even partial credit is better than none. To make a good guess, read each question twice and underline key words. See if there are clues in the surrounding information or in other questions. Make the most of whatever you know about the question.

10. *Check your test.* Do you have an answer to each question? If you have a good reason for doing so, change answers. More answers go from wrong to right than from right to wrong if the test taker makes intelligent changes. Erase smudges and stray marks so your answer sheet looks neat. Correct spelling that looks wrong. Put in any missing punctuation.

Follow-up

1. *Read over corrected tests.* Learn from your mistakes right away, so you know what to do (or not to do) next time. Write a little note reminding

yourself what to be careful about on the next test in that subject.

2. *Relax, it's over.* If you have followed all these steps, enjoy your freedom. Even if you didn't do as well as you had hoped, forget about it until next time. You deserve a break!

2
How To Learn Test Material

Have you ever stared at your heavy textbook, your piles of handouts, and your pages of class notes and wished you knew just what questions your teacher planned to put on the next big test? Lacking a crystal ball, most students feel they have no choice but to plow through *all* that material, drill it into their brains, and hope they can remember the right parts at test time.

That's the hard way to study. If you learn the best ways to take good notes, read a textbook, make up study tools, and memorize, you'll make the job of studying for tests a lot easier from now on.

Taking Good Notes

1. *Keep up with your assigned textbook reading.* When you come to class prepared, your teacher's comments make more sense.

2. Date each day's notes and leave wide margins. Dated notes guide you to the right material to study for a test. At test time, the extra margins give you room to add more information if you need it.

3. Write down main ideas and underline or highlight them. Main ideas give you the "big picture" of information, the reasons why events took place. While the date 1492 isn't a main idea, Columbus's voyage to the New World *is*. The names of his ships aren't main ideas; they are details that fit under the main idea. Class notes on this information might look like this:

	Columbus--new route to riches in Asia
	1492
	Nina, Pinta, Santa Maria

Write out a main idea whenever you think you hear one. Then use single words or short phrases to list related details like dates, names, events, rules, steps, and facts that tie into the big idea. This kind of notetaking helps you connect related chunks of information, making it easier for you to remember it for a test later on.

4. Use abbreviations and symbols to make notetaking easier. Here are a few simple ones:

+	*plus, and*	w	*with*
−	*minus*	w/o	*without*
=	*equal, same as,*	ex. or e.g.	*for example*
	similar, like		

5. *Call attention to important information.* Use stars, underlining, exclamation points, lightning bolts, or highlighting to help you notice important information.

6. *See your teacher or a classmate about confusing notes.* If you write down something that doesn't make sense, talk to someone right away to clear up the problem.

Reading a Textbook

Along with giving you great arm muscles, textbooks contain most of the information you should know in a course, all in one place. Although all that material looks intimidating — and weighs a lot — most textbooks present the information in a way that organizes the information for you. If you take advantage of a textbook's helpful features from the first day you open the book, you'll be able to remember the information at test time without rereading it all over again.

Reading a Textbook the First Time
1. *Read the Table of Contents and the Introduction*

14

the first day you get the book. This gives you the overview, or "big picture," of what the book is all about. Then each time you get a reading assignment, whether it is a chapter or a set of pages, skim the Table of Contents again. This review will help you figure out where new information fits in.

2. *Read all the boldface chapter headings before you read anything else.* Boldface headings organize the new information, break it up into readable sections, and give an overview of the main ideas.

3. *Quickly skim the assigned pages once.* This gives you an overall sense of what the chapter or sections are about.

4. *Read the questions at the end of the chapter.* These questions alert you to the main ideas of the material.

5. *Go back and reread the chapter slowly.* Once you've read the headings, the chapter questions, and skimmed the chapter once, this second, slower reading will make a lot more sense.

6. *Study charts, graphs, maps, and illustrations.* Visual information in a textbook gives you a picture version of the main ideas and a different way to reinforce the information.

7. *Answer the questions at the end of the chapter.* Do this in writing if that is your homework assignment. Even if you are not required to answer the questions on paper, see if you can quickly answer them in your head.

8. *Make up study tools or a study sheet if you have*

time. Ask your parent or teacher to make up plenty of copies of the sheet on pages 17 and 18, or copy it on notebook paper. Use this sheet as a bookmark for each chapter in your textbook, then fill in the information as you read. Just jot down single words and short phrases to make the job easy. The sheet asks you to fill in the boldface headings from each section of a chapter, then summarize main ideas and related facts. If you follow this form, you will have a complete chapter outline to use as a study tool at test time.

BOOKMARK STUDY SHEET

_____   _____
    Name of textbook   Chapter number and title

What's the overall "big idea" of the chapter? In two or three sentences or phrases, in your own words, tell what you think the chapter is about.

I   Boldface section heading (Page ___): _____
_____

    A. Main idea of the section: _____
_____

             Related facts   Importance of fact
      1. _____   _____
      2. _____   _____
      3. _____   _____
      4. _____   _____

II Boldface section heading (Page ___) _____
_____

    A. Main idea of section: _____
_____

             Related facts   Importance of fact
      1. _____   _____
      2. _____   _____
      3. _____   _____
      4. _____   _____

III Boldface section heading (Page ___) _____
_____

    A. Main idea of section: _____
_____

             Related facts   Importance of fact
      1. _____   _____
      2. _____   _____
      3. _____   _____
      4. _____   _____

IV Boldface section heading (Page __) _____
_____

  A. Main idea of section: _____
_____

Related facts	Importance of fact
1. _____	_____
2. _____	_____
3. _____	_____
4. _____	_____

V   Boldface section heading (Page __) _____
_____

  A. Main idea of section: _____
_____

Related facts	Importance of fact
1. _____	_____
2. _____	_____
3. _____	_____
4. _____	_____

VI Boldface section heading (Page __) _____
_____

  A. Main idea of section: _____
_____

Related facts	Importance of fact
1. _____	_____
2. _____	_____
3. _____	_____
4. _____	_____

Possible test questions:
_____
_____
_____
_____
_____
_____

Reviewing a Textbook for a Test

1. *Catch up on any reading you missed.*
2. *Read the Table of Contents.*
3. *Read all boldface headings of material to be covered.*
4. *Slowly read the opening and closing sections of the material to be covered.*
5. *Complete the study sheet on pages 17–18 if you haven't done so, or make up your own study tools.* List main ideas and facts on flash cards, outlines, time-lines, and lists.
6. *Memorize the information in your study tools.*
7. *Answer the questions at the end of the chapter(s) and predict possible test questions, then answer them.*
8. *Reread difficult sections of the material.*

Reading a Work of Fiction

Reading a Work of Fiction for the First Time

Just as you don't have to read a textbook all over again to get ready for a big test, you don't have to reread a work of fiction either if you have read it carefully in the first place. Following is a bookmark study sheet to complete as you read assigned fiction books. See if someone can make extra copies of this to have on hand for each book you read, or copy the study sheet on notebook paper. Fill the sheet out as you go along, and save it for a big test. Since this is for your own use, feel free to use short words, phrases, and page numbers that will trigger your memory at test time.

BOOKMARK STUDY SHEET
FICTION

Name of book: _____ Author: _____

Number each chapter and write a phrase that sums up what happens.

Chapter	What happens in the chapter
_____	_____
_____	_____
_____	_____
_____	_____
_____	_____
_____	_____
_____	_____
_____	_____
_____	_____
_____	_____
_____	_____
_____	_____
_____	_____
_____	_____
_____	_____
_____	_____
_____	_____
_____	_____
_____	_____
_____	_____

List the main characters and a few words about what they are like.

   Main Characters   What he/she is like

_____ _____

_____ _____

_____ _____

_____ _____

_____ _____

What is the problem the main character has to solve? _____

_____

List page numbers of important events in the book for future rereading.

          Important events   Pages

_____ _____

_____ _____

_____ _____

_____ _____

_____ _____

List quotations or page numbers of important quotations and tell why each quotation is important.

_____ _____

_____ _____

_____ _____

_____ _____

What message or idea do you think the author is trying to get across?

_____

_____

Possible test questions:

_____

_____

_____

Reviewing a Work of Fiction for a Test

1. *Catch up on any reading you may have missed.*

2. *Fill out the study chart if you haven't done so already.*

3. *Look up any quotations or pages you have marked on the chart.* Reread those pages or quotations so that you can identify who said them and understand their importance.

4. *Predict and answer questions you think your teacher might ask.* You can do this in your head or with another person.

Making Your Own Study Tools

Study tools are your own personally designed system for remembering information. Flash cards to predict questions, as well as lists, outlines, time-lines, or tapes help you focus on what's important to study. Following is a list of some handy study tools to know about. The best time to make up a study tool is when you first do the work. However, if you don't get to the job then, make up your study tools a few days before a test.

Flash Cards

Gather a pile of index cards or cut some notebook paper into sections. After you've skimmed your class notes and the textbook material that's going to be on a test, search for important ideas, names, events, rules, dates, steps, facts, etc. Write each on one side of the card. Then, *Jeopardy*-style, write the matching question for the fact on the other side. Here are some examples:

Side 1

force that pulls objects toward Earth

leader of the Aztecs

mass and volume

distance around an area

fur trade

Side 2

what is gravity?

who was Montezuma?

what factors affect density?

what is a perimeter?

why did the French send explorers to North America?

As you can see, you can do this quickly in just a few words. When you have all the cards you need, ask yourself each question, then answer it out loud as completely as you can. Predicting test questions like this is a great way to zero in on important material.

How do you know which questions to ask? Look back to the underlined or highlighted parts of your class notes. Find and answer questions at the end of textbook chapters. Think about how you can turn important statements into test questions.

Teachers often create essay questions by pulling out the main idea of each section in a textbook chapter or a set of notes. You can do the same thing by thinking up one main idea question for each long passage in a textbook chapter. Put the question on a list or card, then try to answer it out loud or in your head.

Outlines

An outline uses numbers and letters to group together main ideas and supporting details. Design one of your own by using boldface textbook headings as the main headings of the outline. Fill in the letter sections with details. On the opposite page is an example of how a history chapter might be outlined. You will find a blank outline to copy on pages 80–81 of this book.

CHAPTER 4 OUTLINE

"THE ROAD TO INDEPENDENCE"

I **The Revolution Begins** (This is a section heading in chapter)
  A. Colonists steal British gunpowder — 12/14/1774
  B. Colonists drive back General Gage from Salem
  C. Patrick Henry
    1. "Liberty or Death" speech
    2. Says colonists need militia

II **From Concord to Bunker Hill**
  A. Paul Revere & Wm. Dawes warn of British coming
    1. April 18, 1775
    2. Stop in Lexington, then Concord, Mass.
  B. Colonists drive back Br. soldiers in Concord & Lex.
  C. Ethan Allen takes Ft. Ticonderoga from Brits.
  D. Second Continental Congress
    1. May 10, 1755 — Philadelphia
    2. Hancock, Adams, Franklin, Washington decide to form militia
      a. Washington elected Commander
      b. States agree to this
  E. **Battle of Bunker Hill**
    1. Americans on top of hill fire on Brits.
    2. Over a thousand Brit. soldiers killed
    3. Amer. victory = confidence to continue

Timelines

A timeline is a long or wide strip that lists events in the order in which they happened. A timeline helps you *picture* the order of events and understand how they *connect*. Consider making up a timeline for big history tests in which you will be asked about events and dates.

Here's an example of a short timeline on the American Revolution. You might find it helpful to write out your timeline on long strips of freezer paper or on several sheets of notebook paper taped together horizontally.

1765	1773	1774	1775	1776	1781
Stamp Act	Boston Tea Party	1st Cont. Congress	Battles Lex. Concord	Decl. Ind.	Brits. Surrender

Study Tapes

Tape the information you need to know and listen to it over and over until you have it memorized. Later, tape possible test questions, leave a long pause after each one, then try to answer the questions during the pause. Making study tapes is one of the easiest, most effective ways to memorize and test yourself without writing down a single word!

Other Kinds of Study Tools

EASIER BOOKS:

If you find your textbook material difficult or confusing, go to the young children's section of the library and find a simple book on your text subject. There are wonderful illustrated nonfiction books covering hundreds of areas of science, history, and math, which might help you picture and better understand difficult material.

STUDY GROUPS:

College students often form study groups to help each other prepare for a test. If you want to study with friends, assign each other specific jobs ahead of time: making up study tools, predicting test questions, sharing notes. Make sure each person has done all of his or her work before you meet. Promise to study together for a specific amount of time before you do anything else. Shared studying can work well if you make plans ahead of time and stick to them.

Memorizing

Many students consider memorizing the worst part of preparing for a test, a kind of stuffing-the-brain process. Memorizing doesn't have to be a horrible experience if you think of it as a filing and sorting system instead.

If you've taken clear notes, read material in an organized way, and participated in class discussions, you've been doing some memory work. If you get in the habit of making up your own simple study tools as you go along, you'll have completed the most important part of memorization — zeroing in on important information.

Following is a review of some of the steps covered so far and some additional steps to help you memorize information for a big test:

1. *Schedule memory work for a few short study sessions.* Plan your memory work for the beginning of each study period when your mind is fresh. Do memory work in short spurts — no more than fifteen minutes at a time a couple of days before a test.

2. *Find out what you should memorize.* Ask your teacher what you should memorize. If you can't find out by asking, use your notes, boldface entries in your textbook reading, and lists at the end of chapters to guide you. Usually teachers want you to memorize spelling; definitions; names of people and their achievements; rules; historical, grammatical, or scientific terms; events and their importance; and certain dates.

3. *Understand the meaning of what you want to memorize.* If the textbook explanation or your teacher's explanation doesn't make sense, have someone explain the information in a new way. Or rewrite information in a simpler way that makes sense to

you. Don't just parrot the words; really try to understand what they mean.

4. *Memorize information from your study tools.* The purpose of study tools is to group and organize important information briefly, so that you don't have to plow through all the reading again. So it makes sense to memorize what you consider important enough to include in your study tools.

5. *Tie in new information with what you already know.* Ask yourself where the new facts fit into old ideas and facts you've learned before.

6. *Write down, reread, or say out loud what you want to memorize.* Repeat the information until you can say it back without looking. If you have many items to learn, memorize the first item, then the second. Recite those two items, then add the third. With each new addition, go back to the beginning and recite each item in turn. The hardest items to remember are those in the middle, so spend a little extra time working on those.

7. *Tape record what you want to memorize.* Recite the material you want to memorize into a tape recorder and play it back during your study sessions as well as at other times. This method works especially well for spelling and vocabulary.

8. *Test yourself.* Using a tape recorder or your study tools, recite back what you have memorized, then check it against the original. If you can, have someone quiz you.

3
How To Take
All Kinds of Tests

By now you've probably discovered that there are tests, and there are TESTS! Short, simple quizzes may take only ten or fifteen minutes out of the day and cover just one kind of information, perhaps spelling, vocabulary, or one type of math process. Usually a quick review the night before is all you need to do well on quizzes.

TESTS — the kind you think of with capital letters, exclamation points, and nervous thoughts — cover a lot of different kinds of material in different ways. After this type of exam, your fingers are often cramped from holding a pen or pencil for so long, and you may even feel like you've run a marathon!

Let's take a look at all kinds of tests — from short quizzes to multiple-sheet exams — to see what shortcuts and tips you can use to do a great job on each of them.

Objective Tests

Many tests you're going to get from now on ask questions that have definite right or wrong answers. These are called *objective* tests and include true-false, multiple choice, fill-in, matching items, and short answers. Generally, you should study and memorize *facts and details* for objective tests.

Follow these steps for taking any kind of objective test:

1. Read the directions twice and underline important words that tell you exactly what to do.

2. Find out how many points each question is worth and how much time you have for the test. Allot a couple of minutes at the beginning to skim the whole test, and five minutes at the end to check it over. Divide the remaining time by the number of questions on the test. Schedule more time for more valuable sections.

3. Skim the entire test to get a sense of what it's about and to spot any easy questions.

4. Do the easiest, most valuable questions first to gain quick points. *Mark those you skip with a dot or question mark in the margin*. Read each statement carefully. If you know the answer immediately, you're probably right, so mark your answer.

5. Work on the more difficult questions, but *don't get stuck*. Move on to those you *can* answer, erasing

your margin marks as you finish. Then go back and carefully guess the answers to the questions you don't know.

6. Check over the entire test, including the directions. Make sure you've answered each question. Change an answer if you have a good reason for doing so. Erase any stray or smudge marks.

True-False

True-false questions ask you if a statement is right or wrong.

EXAMPLE:

The Stamp Act of 1765 only taxed the American colonists' letters. True or false? (Answer: *False*)

STUDY METHOD:

Study facts, definitions, and important statements in your reading and class notes. Memorizing is important. The best study tool is a list of important facts with explanations next to each one.

TEST TIPS:

• Underline key words in each true-false statement such as *only*, *some*, *always*, *never*, *all*, *none*, *likely*, *unlikely*, *rarely*, *probably*.

• If one part of a true-false statement is false, the whole statement is false.

• Teachers often include more true than false

statements, since it's easier to pull them out of the textbook.

• If you're not sure of an answer, take a guess, since you have a fifty-fifty chance of being right.

Multiple Choice

This is a kind of true-false test with more choices. Pick the statement that is the *truest* of all the choices.

EXAMPLE:

The Stamp Act of 1765 was created to
   A. punish the American colonists.
   B. raise money for England.
   C. pay for postal service. (Answer: *B*)

STUDY METHOD:

Study statements, dates, definitions, names, and facts that your teacher has mentioned in class or which you've read in your textbook. Try to tie related facts together. Make up flash cards or lists with key words on one side and explanations on the other.

TEST TIPS:

• See if you can figure out the answer *before* you look at the choices, then choose the one that's most like yours.

• Keep in mind that you're looking for the *best* choice, although it may not have the exact wording of the information you have studied.

• Cross out obviously wrong choices to narrow the possibilities.

• Underline key words like: *greatest, smallest, largest, true, untrue*, which may appear in the statement or the choices. Broad words like *all, none, always, never, forever, totally* usually appear in the *incorrect* choices. Limiting words, like *generally, often, frequently, usually, seldom, sometimes* often appear in *correct* answers. Watch out for the word *not*, which can completely change the entire meaning of the statement.

• Search for clues in the surrounding information. If the question asks about a Spanish explorer, for example, you would look for a Spanish-sounding name.

• Look for clues to one question in the other questions.

Fill-in and Sentence Completion

These types of tests ask you to complete a statement with a logical word or phrase included among many answers for other questions.

EXAMPLE:

The Stamp Act of 1765 was passed to __*tax*__ the American colonies.

educate   Boston Tea Party   tax   rebellion

STUDY METHOD:

Review and memorize facts, definitions, explanations, steps, and rules your teacher has emphasized in class or which appear in your textbook. The best study tools — flash cards or lists — show an important fact on one side and the explanation on the other. Test yourself by covering the answer and reading the fact, then seeing how well you can complete the statement.

TEST TIPS:

• Answer the question in your head first, then search for the most similar answer in the choices given.

• Do the easiest examples first to narrow down the later choices.

• Look for words that fit in grammatically with the sentence.

• Sometimes, but not always, the length of the blank is a clue to the correct choice.

Matching

In this type you are asked to connect related ideas, terms, explanations, and definitions. Turn the page for an example.

(B) 1. Redcoats

    A. Organized rebellion to protest tax

(D) 2. Stamp Act

    B. British soldiers

(A) 3. Boston Tea Party

    C. British firing on unarmed colonists

(C) 4. Boston Massacre

    D. Law taxing printed matter in the colonies

STUDY METHOD:

Memorize related facts and ideas in clusters on flash cards and with lists that show an item on one side of the page and an explanation on the other. Pretest yourself by reading important items, then reciting what they are.

TEST TIPS:

• If one column is longer than the other, work from the shorter of the two so you don't waste your time trying to match extra items.

• Do all the examples you are sure of first, crossing off the items you've used as you go along.

• Match like with like — words with their definitions; names with accomplishments, goals, or identification; laws and rules with their purpose; events with their dates, locations, or significance.

• Watch out for extra items teachers often throw in. Eliminate these false choices as soon as you've matched up the easiest pairs.

Short Answer

Short-answer questions ask you to provide your own factual answers to the questions. Unlike the other tests listed so far, the answers aren't provided. Short-answer tests usually ask for definitions or identifications.

EXAMPLE:

Identify the following people and events:

1. Crispus Attucks *was the first black rebel to die in the American Revolution.*

2. The Stamp Act *was an unpopular British law passed in 1765 that placed a tax on all printed materials in the American colonies.*

STUDY METHOD:

Memorize exact definitions and facts from flash cards or a list that shows the fact on one side and its meaning on the other.

TEST TIPS:

• Answer short-answer questions in complete sentences.

• Use the most exact definitions or statements from your class or textbook.

• If you don't know the exact answer, take a guess at part of the answer, writing down as much as you remember about the question.

• Write neatly to be sure your teacher will be able to read your answer. Think before you write so you can say your answer in your head. Use correct spelling, grammar, and punctuation. Erase mistakes rather than crossing them out.

Subjective Tests

While objective questions like true-false, multiple choice, and fill-in have definite right and wrong answers, subjective questions ask you to express opinions and back them up with facts. Objective tests mainly test your memory; subjective ones test your thinking and writing ability as well. You still have to know the facts of the material, but on a subjective test you *use* those facts to back up *main ideas* and your own *opinions*. Big tests such as final exams will often include both kinds of questions, so you have to study main ideas *and* the facts that tie into them.

Essay

Essay questions ask you to write out an idea or your opinion about certain material, and support it with facts. Here are two types of questions about the same subject. The first is an objective multiple-choice question; the second is an essay question.

1. The Stamp Act placed _taxes_ on printed material.

taxes   postage   restrictions

2. What was the Stamp Act? Describe how this Act affected the American colonists. Why did the British repeal the Stamp Act?

Here is a possible essay answer for the second question.

The Stamp Act, passed in 1765, was a tax the British placed on all the printed material in the American colonies. When colonists bought newpapers, applied for marriage licenses, or even obtained birth certificates, they had to pay an extra tax for a small blue stamp that was required on all printed matter.

This little blue stamp constantly reminded the American colonists that they were paying their own money to England without having the full rights of English citizens. The Stamp Act tax, more than any other British action, made the colonists organize themselves against British rule.

Finally, the British repealed the Stamp Act in 1766 because it was so unpopular. But the little blue stamp had already done its damage. The colonists had successfully banded together against British rule.

The basic difference between the two kinds of questions is that the first one asks only *what* a certain fact is. The essay question, too, asks *what* the fact is, but also asks the test taker to discuss *why* this fact is important.

STUDY METHOD:

For an essay test, understanding "big ideas" is more important than memorizing facts. Find out from your teacher what main ideas the test is going to cover. When you review your class notes, highlight ideas your teacher discussed over and over. A couple of nights before your test, read the Table of Contents of your textbook and all the boldface headings in the chapter to be covered on the test. Make up an outline, chart, or timeline using these headings and list related facts underneath them. Predict possible essay-test questions and see how well you can answer them. If possible, have someone ask you these questions so that you can discuss your answers out loud.

ESSAY STEPS:

1. Bring scrap paper to class and ask your teacher if you can use it — or the margins of the test sheet — to make notes once the test starts. Most teachers encourage their students to plan out their essay answers before writing the final version.

2. Find out how many points each question is

worth and how much time you have for the test. Essay questions are usually worth many more points than objective questions and take more time. If an essay question or several essay questions are worth fifty percent of the test, set aside half the test time to work on that part.

3. Read the test directions twice and underline important words that tell you exactly what you're supposed to do. The sample Stamp Act essay question above has three parts, which should be numbered. Underline key words like *how, who, what, when,* and so on as well as key instruction words like these:

Analyze: Write about a subject part by part.

Comment or Discuss: Write your own opinions about a subject and support them with facts.

Compare: Show how two subjects are alike.

Contrast: Show how two subjects are different. Many essay questions ask you to compare *and* contrast. This means you should write about similarities *and* differences.

Define: Explain what a certain word or phrase means.

Describe or Explain: Write about the important features of the subject.

Outline or Trace: Write about how a subject developed, took place, or unfolded step-by-step.

4. Plan your answer. On a scrap of paper or in the margins, make a quick list of *everything* you can

think of about the subject that might be useful. Based on these facts, decide what your main statement will be. Then make a quick mini-outline of the facts by numbering them or writing them in order. Include just those items that tie in with your main statement. Use single words and phrases in the mini-outline.

5. Begin writing your answer. In the first sentence, rephrase the question to answer exactly what is asked. Expand this answer with supporting ideas, details, and facts that you've outlined to back up what you stated at the beginning.

6. Check your answer. Make sure you've answered all parts of the question the way your teacher asked. Check that your sentences are complete and no words are missing. See that your writing is neat, readable, and correct.

TEST-TAKING TIPS:

• Move along from point to point by using connecting words like: *first, second, next, then, in addition, finally, on the other hand, however,* etc.

• Spend the most time on your opening and closing sentences, which make the most important impressions. Your introduction should clearly answer the question. In the middle paragraphs, use ideas, facts, and examples to support your opening statement. Wrap up your essay by echoing what you said in the first sentence in a new way.

- Sound positive about what you think. Plunge right into your opinion and supporting facts so that you sound sure of yourself. Avoid fuzzy expressions like: "I think that," "I believe that," etc.
- If you have time, think a little more about the question. In the sample Stamp Act question, for example, explaining the law answers the question. But writing about what it was like for the colonists to pay a tax to the British for every piece of paper adds a deeper meaning to the answer.
- If you start to run out of time, cut back on details, not main ideas.
- If you don't know the whole answer, make the most of the few things you *do* know to get partial credit.

Short Essay

In this kind of essay question, your teacher expects you to answer just the question that was asked and to support it with one or two important details.

EXAMPLE:

What was the Stamp Act?

The Stamp Act was a law the British passed in 1765 to tax all the printed materials in the American colonies. This unpopular tax was designed to pay for the British upkeep of the colonies but was repealed in 1766.

Notice that this answer emphasizes facts rather than opinions and ideas.

STUDY METHOD:
Make up flash cards or a list of important facts from the material to be covered. Put the fact on one side and the explanation of it on the other. Memorize the information as you would for a multiple-choice or fill-in test, but be prepared to write down your answers in well-developed sentences.

TEST TIPS:
• Quickly follow the first three steps you would use to answer a long-essay test.
• Jot down two or three facts on a scrap of paper.
• Write a sentence for each fact.
• Come right to the point; don't pad your answer.
• Sound definite by directly stating the information you know. Avoid "I think" or "I believe."

Other Kinds of Tests

Open Book
Open-book tests sound easy, and they are if you have studied the main ideas of the material and know *exactly* where to find the information quickly. Ask your teacher what kinds of questions will be asked on the open-book test. Then use the study

methods described in this chapter for the kind of test you're going to get. Reading and rereading boldface headings in a textbook is the best way to familiarize yourself with the location of important information. Bring in slips of paper, yellow stick-on notes, or index cards to mark your place. Use the index to find pages quickly. If your open-book test asks you to answer a long-essay question, follow the same steps you read about in this chapter. When you make your outline, write down numbers of the pages that contain information you want to use.

Oral

Occasionally a teacher may want to test the class on a chapter and give students practice in sharing ideas and information out loud; this is called an *oral* test. Find out whether your teacher plans to ask objective questions like those that might be in a multiple-choice test or whether he or she plans to ask essay-style questions. Use the same study methods as those described in this chapter. However, quiz yourself by answering possible test questions on a tape recorder or with another person.

When your turn comes up in class, make sure you understand the question. Have it repeated if you don't quite understand it the first time. Take a minute or so to compose your thoughts.

When you answer, try to "discuss" rather than

"recite" a string of facts. Imagine you're explaining something interesting to someone who doesn't know a thing about the subject. You may want to use a storytelling tone of voice to help you connect your information. Speak slowly and don't be afraid to pause. This will help you collect your thoughts if you've lost them!

Standardized

Have you ever taken a test that had a question book and a separate sheet covered with small fill-in boxes? Schools all over the country give these kinds of tests, called *standardized* tests, to see how well students are learning. The tests are given in different grades, often third and fifth grades, then later on in high school. Tens of thousands of students throughout a state or even all over the country take exactly the same test, in the same grade, so that all the students can be measured equally. Schools sometimes use the results to place students in different levels of certain courses.

You don't have to worry about standardized tests too much in the middle grades, but it's still a good idea to know a little bit about them so you won't be nervous if your grade is scheduled for them.

Standardized tests in the middle grades usually test your reading, vocabulary, and math skills. More than testing the information stored in your brain, standardized tests measure how well you *use* your brain. While you don't have to study specific material for standardized tests, there are certain things you can do to boost your scores.

• *Listen for directions a few days before the test.* Schools want their students to compare well with other pupils on standardized tests, so many teachers help their classes get ready ahead of time. Your teacher may tell you that he or she will have to be a little more strict about sticking to time limits and keeping the class absolutely quiet during the test. You may find out that you won't be able to ask questions once the test starts. This is because in order to make the test fair, all schools giving the test must have the same conditions.

Teachers are sometimes allowed to give a sample practice test a couple of days ahead. This gives you a chance to ask questions about confusing directions or other parts of the test you don't understand. Your teacher may tell you what you should bring in on the day of the test: usually a few sharpened pencils with good erasers, perhaps a watch, and maybe some blank scrap paper if it's allowed.

• *On test day, arrive a bit early, rested, and fed.* It's hard to sit and write for long stretches of time. A good night's rest, some breakfast, and a few spare minutes are the only preparations you need to make before taking a standardized test.

• *Decide four things before you take the test.*

   1. You won't rush.

2. If you don't know an answer, you'll guess. Usually there are three or four choices; your chances of being right are one in three or four, whereas a blank answer is one hundred percent wrong.
3. You'll make up a schedule and be careful about how many minutes you have, since these tests are strictly timed.
4. You'll match your answer sheet to the questions as you work to see that they line up.

• *Ask any last-minute questions before the test starts.* Your teacher will probably speak more slowly and carefully than usual. This will make it easy for you to pay close attention to directions. Since you won't get a chance to talk once the test is underway, ask your questions beforehand. How long do you have? Can you use scrap paper? If not, is it okay to scribble notes in the question booklet? (Usually you can, since only the answer sheets are graded; the booklets are thrown away.)

• *Read the test directions twice and underline key words.*

• *Skim the whole test quickly to get a sense of it and to see how many different sections there are.*

• *Schedule your time.* Divide the time you have by the number of questions on the test. Leave five to ten minutes for checking over your test.

• *Answer the easiest questions first.*

• *Read each choice.* Standardized questions are

trickier than regular classroom tests. There is often more than one choice that *sounds* or *looks* right. Try out each one. Underline key words to help you focus on what the question is *really* asking.

• *Put an X next to any examples you can't do right away.* Keep moving on to the questions you feel sure about. If you skip a question, skip a number and mark that you skipped it. When you have completed the easiest questions, go back and answer *every* question you skipped. *Don't leave any blanks.* To tackle tough questions, eliminate obviously wrong choices, put the choice into your own words, or use information from parts of the question or the choices to make a good guess.

• *Check your answer sheet.* Line up your answer sheet with the question book. Quickly read each question and make sure your answer matches the right one. Sometimes students lose points because they mark answer number three, for example, next to question number four. That means every answer afterward will be wrong. Standardized tests are corrected by machines. Make sure you have marked each of your answers with a *solid* mark. *Erase all stray marks in the margins and elsewhere.*

4
How To Take Tests
in Different Subjects

Does your brain work like a calculator when it comes to math but jam up on spelling? Most students have one or two subjects they find easier than others, and this goes for tests, too. Different subjects require slightly different study and test-taking methods. So it's a good idea to approach each of your courses in a special way. Here are some study tips to help you prepare for tests in each of your subjects:

Math Tests

Before the Test
• *Know your math facts and math vocabulary inside out.* By the time students get to the middle grades, math facts like addition, subtraction, multiplication, and division should be automatic. If you still stumble over these facts when you do homework or

50

take math tests, spend five minutes a day practicing with inexpensive flash cards.

• *Master each step in math as you study it.* More than most subjects, math builds logically from step to step. If you have trouble with a new part of your math, get help immediately. Ask your teacher, a classmate, a parent, or an older brother or sister to explain difficult math problems more simply until you understand them. Work out a half dozen or so problems to see if you're ready to move on to the next step.

• *Do a few homework problems under test conditions.* That is, give yourself a short amount of time to work out three or four problems.

• *Make your own simple drawings or use real objects to help you picture a math problem.* Draw and label geometric shapes with the numbers you have to calculate. Measure or count real quantities and objects if possible.

• *Keep a math "dictionary" in your notebook.* As you learn new terms and rules, write them down in your notebook. At test time, you will save time memorizing and reviewing terms like *area, diagonal, perimeter,* etc., if they are listed in one place.

• *Pretest yourself before any test.* For weekly quizzes, practice your flash cards and make up three or four problems similar to those you studied in class that week. For big tests, make up two problems for each kind of math process you will be tested on. If you have difficulty with some problems, reread the explanations in your textbook and try out a few more problems of that type.

During the Test

• *Read test directions carefully.* Underline words in the directions that tell you how many problems you have to do, how much time you have, where you are supposed to work out your calculations, and where you should write your answers.

• *Do one step at a time.* While it's great to be able to predict or estimate an answer, always work out each part of the problem.

• *Check your answers by working through the problem again.* If you get a different answer, do the calculations a third time.

• *Use special tips for different kinds of math tests:*

Speed tests: Teachers give these one-minute quizzes, sometimes called "Mad Minutes," to give students quick practice in math facts. Your goal is to finish correctly as many examples as possible. The key to doing well is to *keep moving*. Don't get stuck; move on to the next example and go back to finish if you have time.

Computation tests: Like the Mad Minute quizzes, computation exams test your addition, subtraction, multiplication, and division skills but give you a longer time to work out the problems. If you have time, and the problem is fairly simple, estimate the answer, then work out the problem step by step.

Word-problem tests: These can be the trickiest kinds of math tests. Most students like the "real world" visual aspects of word problems, which often deal with quantities of time, money, and real objects. Read word problems very carefully. Look how tricky this simple-looking problem is:

If you take four eggs from a dozen, how many eggs do you have?

The answer is *four*, though someone working too quickly might think it's *eight*. The question does not ask how many are left, simply how many you have. *Figure out what a word problem is really asking.* Here's another kind of tricky word problem:

The photographer lined up three boys and five girls in back of a row of three girls and four boys standing two feet in front of the six-foot wall. How many more students would the photographer need to make the rows even? (Answer: *one more student*)

In this problem the key words, *more students*, should be underlined. Once that's understood, the information about the distance and height of the walls can be ignored.

- *Use math symbols for words.* Here is a list:
  1. Use an equal sign "=" when you see these words: *is/are/was, equal to, has/had, same as.*
  2. Use a plus sign "+" when you see these words: *and, gained, give, get, more than, has/had, so many minutes/weeks/months/years from now.*
  3. Use a minus sign "−" when you see these words: *borrowed, decreased, gave away, less, lost, owe, take from, so many minutes/weeks/months/years ago.*
  4. Use a multiplication sign "×" when you see these words: *of, double, triple,* etc., *percent.*
  5. Use a division sign "÷" when you see these words: *half, thirds, quarters,* etc., *divided.*
  6. *Less than* can be shown as: <
  7. *More than* can be shown as: >

- *When multiplying numbers with many zeros at the end, cancel the zeros and multiply the remaining digits. Add on the missing zeros to your answer.*

EXAMPLE:

$$\begin{array}{r} 12{,}000 \\ \times\,8{,}000 \\ \hline 96{,}000{,}000 \end{array} \qquad \begin{array}{r} 12 \\ \times\,8 \\ \hline 96 \end{array}$$

96 (then add on the six missing zeros to get 96,000,000)

- *Use specific numbers in all-word problems.*

EXAMPLE:

Susan wears larger shoes than Melissa, who wears larger shoes than Eileen. Who wears the smallest shoes?

Imagine Susan wears size 7 shoes; Melissa, size 6; Eileen, size 5. Therefore Eileen wears the smallest shoes.

Literature Tests

Before the Test
- *Fill out the bookmark study sheets on pages 20 and 21 as you read.* Pay attention to important quotations your teacher has discussed. Make sure you can identify the quotations and explain their importance and meanings.
- *Be able to tell the plot of the story in some detail.*
- *Memorize two or three quotations that reveal something important about the main character or the spirit of the book.* Have these quotations in mind and work them into any related essay questions.

During the Test
- *First, skim any reading passages once to get a sense of what it is about.*
- *Next, skim questions about the passage.*

• *Then* reread *the passage slowly, looking for details to help answer the questions.*

Grammar Tests

How to Study
• *Memorize grammar rules from flash cards or a list.*

• *Be able to say or write one sentence that uses the grammar rule.*

• *Skim the homework grammar exercises.* Your teacher will probably use similar examples on the test. Do two examples from each exercise.

• *Study related grammar rules*, that is, study all the pronoun rules together, punctuation rules, etc.

Vocabulary Tests

Before the Test
• *Memorize the words your teacher says will be covered.* Use flash cards or lists with the words on one side and the definitions on the other and recite them back until you can say them by heart. If you have a tape recorder, tape the words and their definitions and play them back until you can "hear" them in your head.

• *Pretest yourself.* Have someone quiz you out loud on the vocabulary definitions or make up a list of the words and say their definitions out loud.

Make up a sentence in which you use the word.

- *Know these key words ahead of time*
  Synonym: a word that has nearly the *same* meaning as another.
  Antonym: a word that has nearly the *opposite* meaning as another.
  Homonym: a word that looks and sounds the same as another but has a different meaning, such as *brake* and *break.*

During the Test

- *Be alert to tricky parts of the question.* Underline or circle phrases like: "Choose the word that is *least like,*" "*most like,*" "*same as,*" or "*opposite to.*"
- *Guess the answer in your head,* then see if there's a similar choice in the possible answers.
- *Use clues in the surrounding words to figure out the meaning.*
- *Try out each choice to see how it sounds.*

Analogy Tests

Analogies present two pairs of two different words that show similar relationships. Analogy questions test both your vocabulary and your skill in seeing how very different words can be related. Here is an example:

CARPENTER : SAW   DOCTOR : STETHOSCOPE

Can you see the relationship? The first part of each pair shows a kind of worker. The second half shows a tool that worker might use. On an analogy test, the question might be shown like this:

CARPENTER : SAW ::
- A. MECHANIC : CAR
- B. DOCTOR : STETHOSCOPE
- C. AUTHOR : NOVEL
- D. WRENCH : PLUMBER

During the Test

Follow the usual strategies for test taking — careful reading of directions, scheduling time, skimming, working on easy problems before harder ones, rechecking.

• *Turn the analogy into a sentence to complete the analogy.* A CARPENTER is a working person. A SAW is a tool.

• *Turn each analogy choice into a sentence.*

A. A MECHANIC is a worker. A CAR is a machine, therefore not a tool. Wrong answer. Try the next choice.

B. A DOCTOR is a worker. A STETHOSCOPE is a tool. Good choice but quickly try the others.

C. An AUTHOR is a worker. A NOVEL is the work produced. Wrong answer.

D. A WRENCH is a tool. A PLUMBER is a worker. However, the relationship must be shown in

the same order as the question, so this is a
wrong answer.

Example B is the correct answer.

Here is a list of relationships that are often used
in analogies:

Synonyms	HAPPINESS : JOY
Antonyms (opposites)	LAUGHTER : SOBS
Whole to its part	SKELETON : RIB
Object to its purpose	OAR : ROW
Raw material to product	WOOD : CHAIR
Group to individual	CAT : SIAMESE
Female to male	DOE : BUCK
Singular to plural	MOUSE : MICE

Spelling Tests

Before the Test

• *Memorize your spelling list.* Write out the words,
tape record them, or repeat the spellings out loud
until you know them. Learn the spelling of troublesome words by dividing them into syllables.

• *Keep an ongoing list of your own spelling demons.*
Some words are always trouble. Checking these
occasionally is one way to master them.

• *Learn spelling rules.* Here are some common
ones:

   1. Drop the final *e* before a suffix that begins
   with a vowel. Examples: *take + ing = taking;
   move + able = movable.* Exceptions: If the *e* is

preceded by a soft *c* or *g* sound, keep the final *e*. Examples: *notice* + *able* = *noticeable; change* + *able* = *changeable.*

2. When the suffixes *less* and *ly* are added, the root word remains the same. Examples: *care* + *less* = *careless; usual* + *ly* = *usually.*

3. When the prefixes *dis, il, im, in, mis, over, re,* and *un* are added, the root word remains the same. Examples: *dis* + *able* = *disable; il* + *legal* = *illegal; im* + *balance* = *imbalance; in* + *dependent* = *independent; mis* + *fortune* = *misfortune; over* + *hand* = *overhand; re* + *cover* = *recover; un* + *able* = *unable.*

4. When the vowel sound in a word is *ee,* the *e* follows the *i* except when right after *c.* Examples: *achieve, believe, relieve* (but *receive*).

5. When the vowel sound is not pronounced *ee,* the spelling is usually *ei.* Examples: *foreign, veil, freight, weight.* Some exceptions: *friend, handkerchief, sieve.*

• *Pretest yourself.* Have someone quiz you or use your tape recorder to quiz yourself. Copy or recite the spellings of words you get wrong until you know them.

• *During the test, listen, spell the word in your head, write it, check it.*

• *Put a mark in the margin for words you are unsure about.*

• *Recheck your paper.*

History and Social Studies Tests

Before the Test

• *Get an overview of the time period you are studying.* Review the Table of Contents and boldface chapter headings.

• *Tie in the facts you have to memorize with main ideas.* Learn information for a test in connection with major events.

• *Make up your own study tools.* Use the bookmark study sheet for your textbook materials in history and geography. Make up a timeline of historical events. In geography, draw or trace the shape of the land you are studying, then see how well you can label the map with geographical features like rivers, mountains, bodies of water, etc., or cities, capitals, and borders.

During the Test

• *When you answer essay questions, follow the time sequence that is mentioned in the question.*

Science Tests

Before the Test

• *Save all your lab notes.* Laboratory experiments help you picture and remember scientific processes.

• *Find children's simple books on the subject you are studying.* Get one or two very simple science books with plenty of pictures to get a good understanding of difficult science material. Usually picture books illustrate and explain the same material more clearly than a textbook.

• *Relate the information to real life.* If you're studying density and mass, find everyday objects that show examples of this. For example, a golf ball is denser than a tennis ball. If you have that comparison in mind at test time, the concept of density will be easier to recall.

• *Predict and pretest yourself with these kinds of questions:*

  1. Define a certain science term.
  2. How does a particular object work?
  3. What are the qualities or properties of that object?
  4. Draw or label the object. (Try to draw or trace the object(s) you're studying; simple line drawings are fine. Then see if you can label it yourself.)

Foreign Language Tests

Before the Test

• *Learn the grammar of your own language inside out.* A lot of foreign language courses take for granted a student's knowledge of grammatical terms like nouns, verbs, tenses, etc.

• *If possible, use a tape recorder to review for a test.*

Reading, saying, and hearing words in a foreign language reinforce its meaning in several ways. Even if you hate your accent or feel silly, do as much review work as you can out loud.

• *Make up flash cards or a list with the English word on one side and the foreign language word on the other.* Use these study tools to test yourself.

• *Read children's foreign language storybooks from your library.* Most libraries have a few shelves of well-known children's folk and fairy tales in different foreign languages. These are often fun to read. When you know the plot and characters already, it's easy to figure out the meaning of new words without worrying about vocabulary and grammar the way you might in your regular class work. Try it.

During the Test

• *Skim foreign language material once to get a sense of it.* You will understand more than you think if you don't get bogged down defining words or working out the grammar as you go along. Ask yourself, What is this passage about?

• *Go back and underline, then try to translate troublesome words.* If you can, scribble in your translation above difficult words.

• *To translate, rely on words that look and mean the same in English and the foreign language.*

• *Reread the passage slowly.*

• *Use information from the question or passage to help you figure out the answer*. For example, if a question on your French test asks about a fisherman in Brittany, look in the passage for the word *Bretagne* to help you locate the answer.

5
Test-Taking
Problems and Solutions

Do you think you're the only student who puts off studying as long as possible? Do you wonder if other kids get butterflies or freeze up at the sight of a test sheet? Do you swallow hard when the good grade you hoped for turns out to be something else? If you've ever had any of these feelings, then you're like a lot of other students in the middle grades who feel very mixed up about taking tests.

Here is what other middle-schoolers worry about when it comes to tests.

Procrastinating

PROBLEM: *Even though I know I could do better if I studied ahead of time, I always wind up studying for tests just the night before. Why do I keep doing this and how can I stop?*

SOLUTION: Kids, and a lot of grown-ups, too, often put things off because they want to do a perfect job! Strange as that sounds, psychologists who have done research on the reasons people procrastinate — put things off — have found that many procrastinators have very high expectations. As long as they don't get started on whatever the job is — a project, a paper, a test — they can go along thinking they are going to do a perfect job.

Sitting down and actually working spoils that fantasy. The procrastinator finds out he or she doesn't know all the science steps, the math rules, or the spelling words. By waiting until the last minute, a procrastinator who winds up doing a less-than-perfect job can hang onto the fantasy by saying: "Well, if only I had studied sooner, I would have gotten an A+." The solution is for the procrastinator to start thinking instead: "I'm going to make an A+ effort."

If this sounds like part of the reason you put things off, tell yourself an A+ *try* is a lot more important than an A+ test result. The bonus is that by actually making that A+ try, you *will* increase your chances of getting that good grade after all.

Some people put things off when a job seems too big to handle. The solution is to view any job — whether it's cleaning your room or taking a test — as a series of much smaller jobs. Instead of thinking about the heavy textbook that seems to grow larger in size the minute your teacher announces a test, forget about the textbook for a few days. Instead, spend the first night the week before the test just making up a study schedule and nothing else. The next night, set aside fifteen minutes or so just to highlight important ideas in your notes with a marker. Maybe the third night, just scribble out an outline or make up a set of index cards on your history facts. Now you have actually done *something* about the test. The great thing about working through the small stuff is that soon the big job is almost finished. So the next time you find out a big test is scheduled, make yourself sit down for even just five minutes that day and do *one* small thing. Do one small thing every day, and before you know it, you'll be ready for the test.

Cramming

PROBLEM: *I know cramming is bad, but what if something happens, and I have to?*

SOLUTION: You mean like being snowbound without your books the week or month before your test? Okay, it happens. Maybe you get sick, or some family problems upset your study schedule. If you have been doing your schoolwork all along, especially following the study strategies for reading and notetaking in Chapter 2, then you should be somewhat test-ready no matter what.

The advice for cramming only works if you are up-to-date on your reading and notetaking. (If you're not, then the only thing you can do is take the test, do the best you can, and then be sure to get yourself up-to-date before the next one.)

If you *have* to cram, here's how to do it:

• Find the quietest spot in your house and shut the door.

• Read all your notes and class handout sheets once.

• Make a list of important facts and ideas as you read.

• Read the headings and the first and last paragraphs of each section in the material you are going to be tested on.

• There's no time to memorize, so don't try. Just read possible test items three times out loud, preferably into a tape recorder so you can replay it back when you brush your teeth before going to bed!

• Ask yourself the questions at the end of your textbook chapter. If the test is on math, make up a half dozen problems and work them out quickly.

• Go to bed at your usual time. Losing sleep will only make it harder for you to concentrate during your test. Get a good night's sleep.

• Get to class early and try to relax. Use every test-taking skill you know to increase your success on the test. Concentrate on building up what you do know by working hard on the most valuable, easy questions.

- When it's all over, promise yourself not to cram again. A little day-by-day studying makes your school life a lot easier than stuffing your brain at the last minute.

Concentration

PROBLEM: *When it comes to studying, I can't sit still. I have to walk around, play with the dog, get up for a glass of water, daydream, do anything but study. How can I concentrate better?*

SOLUTION: Lots of kids imagine that top students work inside some kind of quiet tomb and do nothing else for long stretches of time. If that's the picture you have of ideal study conditions, that's probably why you can't sit still. Let's take a look at a realistic setting — like the average student's busy, noisy home and school — to see how to work in it.

When you make your study schedule, plan some time for fun, too. If you know you'll have plenty of time for television, playing with the dog, or getting a snack later on, you'll find it easier to sit still for short periods of time. In the week before a big test, look over the television schedule and mark down what you most want to watch. Then plan around that. If daily phone calls are important to you, decide when you're planning to study and ask your friends to call at other times.

You don't need perfect quiet to do some parts of test preparation. The kitchen table is a fine place to make up your study tools — flash cards, out-lines, study lists, etc. However, when you actually begin memorizing the information on them, go to the quietest part of your house and shut the door.

Rereading notes and material should also take place at a quiet time in a quiet place. How about during a study period at school? If you share a room, see if there's a time you can reserve it for yourself. Do your memorizing and reviewing then.

Once you've started studying, if you get up, get right back down. If you call in the dog, send him away after a minute. If you start daydreaming, give yourself one minute to finish the dream, then get back to work. If you can't seem to resist cleaning out your closet all of a sudden, just straighten up your shoes and get back on track. In short, if you just *have* to let off a little tension, do it for a limited amount of time to get it out of your system, then hit the books again.

Nervousness

PROBLEM: *Just hearing about a big test coming up ruins my life until it's over. I feel as if I have to study everything ten times and forget about the rest of my life. How can I take it easy and still do well?*

SOLUTION: Believe it or not, the solution to your problem is the same cure that procrastinators should follow. Break down your study job into the small steps described in Chapter 1 and in the Test-Taking

Checklist in Chapter 6. Each of the steps shows a different way to remember material so that you don't have to keep rereading your notes and textbooks over and over. Highlighting, reading headings, and making up simple study tools work just as well as overreading material, and take a lot less time.

Sickness

PROBLEM: *Is it a good idea to go in on test day if you feel sick? One time I did that and I practically fell asleep on my test!*

SOLUTION: Get plenty of rest and eat healthy foods in the days before a big test. Steady studying a little at a time is good preventive medicine so that you don't burn yourself out with late hours and mixed-up mealtimes. However, if you wake up on test day feeling sick, stay home. You will do a lot better on your big test if you schedule a makeup as soon as you get back to school. You don't have to start studying all over again. Just do a quick review of your study tools or notes before the makeup test.

Freezing Up

PROBLEM: *I do my work pretty well all year long and don't have problems studying, but my heart races a mile a minute the second I walk into class on test day. Sometimes my brain just freezes after I get the test, and*

I can't think of one single thing I studied. How can I relax?

SOLUTION: Start relaxing the night before by lining up your school things and going to bed on time. Promise yourself not to study or review at all on the day of the test. If you are prepared already, you shouldn't have to study at the last minute. Take your time having a good breakfast in the morning. If you have free time before the test, read something totally unrelated to that subject or just relax with some of your friends. Get to class a little early if you can and slow down your breathing. Tightening, then relaxing leg muscles is a soothing exercise you can do while waiting for the teacher to hand out the test. Doodling is another way to release tension while you wait.

If you still freeze up when you get the test, stop thinking about the material for a minute and think of something peaceful — lying in the sun, taking a warm bath, being indoors on a stormy day. If you are still stuck, then move through the test steps recommended in this book: Skim the whole test, find the easiest question, and do that one first. Once you complete that, you will get the wheels turning for the rest of the test.

Running Out of Time

PROBLEM: *Sometimes I lose points because I have trouble finishing tests. How can I work faster?*

SOLUTION: Don't work faster; work better. Here are a few things to try. Wear a watch to class and lay it down on your desk where you can't miss it. When the test starts, scribble out a schedule on scrap paper or at the top of the test sheet, then stick to it. Plan your schedule by dividing the time you have by the number of questions on the test. Figure in extra time for the most valuable questions and for checking over your test. Skim the entire test, then go straight to the easiest of the most valuable questions. Because they are easy, you will probably have time left over for the more difficult questions. Many test takers who have problems finishing tests on time simply spend too much time on certain questions. So always move quickly through those you do know and don't get stuck on what you don't know.

Finals

PROBLEM: *I do okay on tests when they are spread out. But we have a week of final exams twice a year, and I have a hard time studying so many subjects at the same time. What should I do next time?*

SOLUTION: Final exams *are* pretty intimidating. The key to studying for finals is to make up a month-long study schedule. That may seem like a lot, but use the first couple of weeks to catch up on any reading or notes you missed. Use the Study Planner on pages 82 and 83 to schedule your work.

Allot extra study time for harder courses. Once you have your schedule, do the steps little by little so you spread out the work. Make sure you leave time to do the things you normally enjoy, scheduling them around your study plans as a reward.

Poor Test Scores

PROBLEM: *When I get a bad grade on a test, I sometimes rip up my paper so I never have to look at it again. What's worse is that I get discouraged about that subject, and it gets harder than ever. What should I do about a bad grade?*

SOLUTION: Learn from it. Correct every test you get, either by fixing it when the teacher reviews the test or when you get home. See what the problems are. Write a little note to yourself at the bottom of the test telling yourself what to work on next time. Maybe you misread the test questions or got stuck on one kind of problem. Concentrate on those areas next time. Notice what you did well so you can repeat your success on the next test.

That covers the test part. Keep in mind that tests are only one part of the work you do. Homework, projects, and class participation are other ways to strengthen your overall grade for a course. If you do your work carefully and steadily all along, one low test score isn't going to pull down your grade that much.

Ask your teacher if it's possible to do some extra-credit work to balance out the low grade. Your teacher will remember your extra effort at report card time. If the class work is just too hard, talk to your teacher. Maybe you could use some short-term tutoring to get on track. Or maybe you just had a bad day, something that happens to every student once in a while. Look over the test to learn from it, put it away to use as a study tool next time, and forget it. Everyone makes mistakes.

Exams and quizzes only test knowledge; they don't test *you*, the person. No matter how you do on a test, you are still one of the star baseball players in your neighborhood. Or the good friend who always knows how to say the right thing. Or the best storyteller in your family.

The bad news is that you've got a lot of tests ahead of you. The good news is that you've got a lot of tests ahead of you — and a lot of chances to show what you know.

Above all, you have lots of other situations in which to prove yourself. Every time you help your little brother tie his shoes, every time you listen to your best friend complain for the millionth time about having to wear glasses, every time you make a basket, feed your cat, finish a puzzle or a book, you have passed an important test. Good luck with these and all the tests you take.

6
Test Survival Kit

Test-Taking Checklist

Studying for a Test

☐ Find out what material is going to be covered on the test.

☐ Copy the test date onto a big calendar.

☐ Plan a study schedule so that you do a little each day. Set aside a longer amount of time on the two nights before the test.

☐ Catch up on missing assignments and notes right away.

☐ Make up study tools like lists, outlines, flash cards, etc.

☐ Skim your class notes and handout sheets.

☐ Skim all of your old tests and homework assignments.

☐ Skim your textbook chapters.

☐ Answer in your head questions at the end of chapters.

- [ ] Do your memorizing a little bit at a time, a couple of nights before the test.
- [ ] Think of a few questions the teacher might ask and answer them in your head.
- [ ] Quiz yourself the night before, or study with a friend and quiz each other.
- [ ] Go to bed on time. Have a good breakfast on test day. Take to school what you will need.

Taking the Test
- [ ] Arrive a little early with all your materials — extra paper, two pens, two pencils, and an eraser.
- [ ] Listen carefully to the teacher's directions.
- [ ] Write your name and the date on the test sheet.
- [ ] Read carefully any written directions, underlining important words as you read.
- [ ] Figure out a quick schedule of how much time to spend on each question. Devote more time to questions that are worth the most.
- [ ] Leave a few minutes at the end for rereading the test.
- [ ] Work on the easiest examples first. (However, if some sections are worth more than others, do the easiest of the most valuable questions first.)
- [ ] Go back to the harder questions. If you don't know the answers, make guesses.

☐ When you have finished, check that you did each question.

☐ Change answers if you have a good reason to do so.

☐ Reread the test to make sure you haven't made any mistakes.

☐ Check that your paper is neat and easy to read.

☐ Save all your tests to learn from your mistakes. Old tests make good study sheets for final exams.

Memorizing Checklist

☐ Do your memorizing at the beginning of your study time.

☐ Make sure you understand the material before you try to memorize it.

☐ Write down what you want to memorize. *Or:* Repeat out loud what you want to memorize until you can recite it back automatically. *Or:* If you have a tape recorder, use it to help in memorizing.

☐ Read what you want to memorize into a tape recorder and keep playing it back. *Or:* Quiz yourself on tape.

☐ Keep rereading what you want to memorize until you can "see" it in your mind.

☐ Have a family member quiz you on what you've memorized.

Outline Form

Topic: _____

  I. _____

    A. _____

      1. _____

      2. _____

    B. _____

      1. _____

      2. _____

  II. _____

    A. _____

      1. _____

      2. _____

    B. _____

      1. _____

      2. _____

  III. _____

    A. _____

      1. _____

      2. _____

    B. _____

      1. _____

      2. _____

IV. _____
   A. _____
      1. _____
      2. _____
   B. _____
      1. _____
      2. _____
V. _____
   A. _____
      1. _____
      2. _____
   B. _____
      1. _____
      2. _____
VI. _____
   A. _____
      1. _____
      2. _____
   B. _____
      1. _____
      2. _____

One-Week Study Planner*

Test in: _____ Test Date: _____

Type of questions on test: _____

Textbook material to study: _____

Class notes, homework, old tests
from: _____ to _____

Study tools I should make: _____

Sunday	Monday	Tuesday	Wednesday

*For final exams, copy extra sheets for each week beforehand.

Thursday	Friday	Saturday

Test Record Sheet

Course	Type of Test	Date

Grade	Strong and Weak Points

INDEX

Notetaking: *see* class notes

Objective tests
  types, 31–38
One-week study planner (form), 82–83
Open book tests, 44–45
Oral tests, 45–46
Outlines, 7, 19, 22, 24–25, 40, 42, 45, 67
  form, 80–81

Preparation for tests: *see* under specific types of tests; *see
  also* studying
Procrastination, 65–67

Questions
  essay, 24, 40–42, 61
  fill-in, 31, 34–35
  found in textbooks, 7–8, 15, 19, 24, 68
  hints from teachers on, 5–6, 40, 44–45
  matching, 31, 35–37
  math, 50–55
  objective, 31–38
  on standardized tests, 48–49
  order of answering, 10, 31, 49, 58, 72, 73
  predicting, 19, 22, 24, 40, 62
  short answer, 37–38
  subjective, 38–44
  true-false, 32–33

Reading: *see* textbooks
Running out of time: *see* time organization
Reviewing: *see* studying

Schedules for studying: *see also* time organization; 5–8, 67,
  69, 73–74
  one-week study planner (form), 82–83